CASSANDRA'S CLASSROOM

INNOVATIVE
SOLUTIONS
FOR
EDUCATION
REFORM

CASSANDRA'S CLASSROOM

INNOVATIVE SOLUTIONS FOR EDUCATION REFORM

NANCY DEVLIN, PhD

authorHOUSE®

AuthorHouse™
1663 Liberty Drive
Bloomington, IN 47403
www.authorhouse.com
Phone: 1-800-839-8640

Published by AuthorHouse   08/30/2012

ISBN: 978-1-4772-5299-4 (sc)
ISBN: 978-1-4772-5298-7 (e)

Library of Congress Control Number: 2012913485

Visit
www.Cassandrasclassroom.com
For additional solutions

CONTENTS

Introduction

Teachers are being treated more and more like Cassandra from Greek myth. Cassandra, as the story goes, could foresee the future correctly. Her curse was that no one believed her.

I feel like a Cassandra. I have taught elementary school, grades 1-8, junior college and college courses. I have earned a PhD in educational psychology, and worked twenty years as a school psychologist. I wrote columns on education for twelve years. I believe I know the answers to the problems in education today or at least the right questions to ask. I believe many teachers and parents know the answers and the questions but only outside experts (mainly non-teaching men) are believed.

Reading these articles may give you insights which will enable you to be part of the solution and not part of the problem.

Teaching is a Profession

A school system could have the most modern building, the most up-to-date equipment, the most conscientious school board, the most innovative superintendent and the most caring principal but if it does not have capable teachers, it will not be successful and children will not get the best education that they deserve.

Reformers propose to improve the teaching profession by adding the rank of master teacher and by granting merit pay to a select few. The concept of a master anything is from the trades not professions. A tradesman is first an apprentice, than a journeyman, and finally a master practitioner. In a profession, for example, medicine, a person is first an intern than a doctor. There are no master doctors. If we do not believe that a person given the title of doctor has mastery of his profession, then we would not entrust him with our health care. The same attitude should be true of teachers.

We do not permit doctors to work with patients unsupervised until they have put in a long internship usually with doctors who are at the top of their professions. Minds are as important as bodies yet we permit teachers to take over a class unsupervised in many cases after only one semester of student teaching. As a student teacher, the student may not work with the teachers who are at the top of their profession. In many cases, teachers view supervising student teachers as an extra burden. The evaluation of the students is usually not done by the teachers in the school but by supervisors from the university or college the students attend.

Now is the time to initiate a change in this system, mainly because it is inadequate and does not produce the best teachers. The following is just one example of possible changes in the profession which would result in attracting and keeping the best.

All candidates would graduate from college with an academic major, not an education major. They would learn how to become a capable teacher through an internship in the school system. The candidates for an internship would be required to pass an examination, much like the Law School Admission Test. The test would be developed not only to evaluate the candidate's academic competence but also to measure some of the qualities both personal and emotional, which distinguish the good teacher. In choosing interns, the staff of the school system should have enough information to enable them to select candidates who would enhance the diversity of the staff already in place.

The successful candidates would then enter a two-year internship in the school under the supervision of tenured teachers. Interns would be paid, and, during these two years, they would have an opportunity to discover whether they have the talent, the gift and the love of teaching necessary to be successful in the profession.

During these two years, the tenured teachers would become knowledgeable about whether the candidate should be admitted to the profession or be counseled to leave it. Many people stay in teaching even when they dislike it and are unsuccessful because they have too much invested to leave. This system allows the candidate to leave without losing anything. He still has a college degree with an academic major and a chance to pursue other careers.

On the senior teachers' recommendation, a promising intern would be offered a second two-year contract. During this period the intern would continue to work under supervision, but would be in charge of a class. At the end of these four years, a mandatory tenure decision would be made after careful deliberation by the tenured staff. These teachers would have observed the intern in the classroom and would have compiled any information needed to make the decision. In essence, it is similar to the procedure followed by university faculties.

The concept of merit pay is damaging because many deserving teachers may not get it and they could become discouraged not so much because of the money involved but because of the lack of recognition for their efforts. The competition for merit pay could consume most of the teacher's time, and it has the potential for turning classroom teaching into show business productions. What makes a teacher good is not showmanship but consistency of performance. The good teacher establishes a high level of competency and does not deviate from that level day by day and year by year. To know if a teacher is consistently good takes time. It cannot be done with one or two observations.

One of the greatest problems in education is the unevenness of the abilities of the teachers. A few inadequate teachers affect the output of the whole school and make it harder for the good teacher to function well and produce learners. Critics of education often point to these inadequate teachers and condemn the whole teaching profession. But why blame the teachers for this? They have no voice in the appointment or granting of tenure to new teachers. They did not make the poor tenure decisions: administrators did. The sad part is the administrators tend to move up and out of the school while the teachers are left to cope as best they can with these poor decisions.

The main goal of everyone connected with the school should be the optimum development and functioning of all of the staff and students. After all, schools are in the business of education. This should mean the education of everyone involved. It is a group effort, and if one member of the group fails, they all must take responsibility for this failure. In the same way, take credit for the successes. As things now stand, it is usually the principal or superintendent who is congratulated and honored for the school's successes. This seems strange when it is the teachers who are the backbone of the school system. When they are successful, we all benefit, but especially the children. Now is the time to put into place a system which will ensure more successes.

Attracting Competent People to the Teaching Profession

One of the problems involved in attracting competent people into education may be that it is the only profession which does not have "perks". A perquisite, according to the dictionary, is a privilege or profit incidental to regular wages or salary.

Companies pay for their employees to take courses to upgrade their skills. Many universities give sabbatical leaves of a year every seven years. Many companies routinely give cash bonuses, usually at Christmas and Easter time. These extras are not considered part of a person's salary so the discrepancy between teachers' salaries and other professionals may be greater than originally thought.

Bright young people are beginning to be attracted to the teaching profession in spite of the salary discrepancies. The problem is they will not stay because teaching is essentially a dead-end job. The only avenue for advancement is administration.

The California Commission on the Teaching Profession solved this problem in a report entitled: "Who Will Teach Our Children?" This report gave recommendations on three topics: Restructuring the teaching career and establishing professional standards, redesigning the school as a more productive workplace for teachers and students, and recruiting capable men and women into teaching. One of the most interesting parts of the report was the section entitled "The Story of a Career", in this part, the committee attempted to show how their recommendations would change the teacher of the future.

In this scenario, the teacher was paid by a fellowship program to pursue her training in chemistry. The program offered her one year of college tuition for each year of commitment to teach. She also received pay for a work-study program in which she worked as a tutor and aide in science classes in high school while attending college. As a prospective teacher, she was paid for a summer of intensive course work. At the end of this time, she took and passed competency tests to become a teacher.

She received tenure after three years and paid off her fellowship. After three years of teaching she was ready to pursue graduate work. She was able to do so because her school functioned on a quarter system and offered teachers the possibility of working on ten, eleven or twelve month contracts.

She passed a rigorous examination and became board certified. This meant a raise in salary. After several years, she received training as a peer evaluator and spent a year doing this. The next year, she returned to the classroom. She applied for the sabbatical program which allowed her to take courses for state certification as a mentor teacher and to work part-time at the research facility of a local corporation. After certification, she received a raise in salary and divided her time between her own classes and the classrooms of residents and other teachers she was helping.

She was now an esteemed educator. She served as an adjunct professor at the university, and was the recipient of professional awards. Her income, like that of other senior mentor teachers, equaled that of the school administrators. She took time off for a year to work on school-based staff development and then returned to the classroom. After twenty-five years in teaching, she could negotiate her duties each year. The district sought to use her expertise where it was most needed. She retired at 60, but continued to consult part time with the district and to serve on state-level committees.

This "Story of a Career" ended by the teacher feeling proud of her accomplishments and her life time of service. She chose a profession that offered her excitement, variety, challenge, growth in competence, income, and esteem of the community, her colleagues, and her students. Not many professions can offer those perks.

How Does Your School System
Evaluate its Teachers

In order for your child to receive the education he is entitled to, you need to know how your school system chooses and evaluates its teachers.

A district may have award winning physical facilities, the most expensive books and the latest hot off the press innovative programs, and the smallest class size, but if it does not have good teachers, than your child's education is in jeopardy. Good school systems know this and spend a great deal of time and effort recruiting and hiring the best teachers available.

These systems appoint a committee consisting not only of administrators but of teachers and parents who have been trained to recognize the qualities they want in a teacher who would enhance the educational program in their district.

The first step the committee takes is to screen the applications of a large pool of potential candidates. They then do an intensive evaluation of the group who survived this screening.

The committee holds personal interviews with the remaining candidates and reviews their references. The review should include contacting the previous school. This review often involves talking personally to the person who wrote the reference. In the case of teachers who are recent graduates, the committee inquires about the program they were trained in, its educational philosophy and the quality of the professional staff.

When a tentative rank-ordering of the candidates has been made, the committee's next step is to start with the top candidate and to observe her teaching. The committee members have been trained to do this well. They understand that this is the most crucial step in the whole process because a teacher may talk a good line and tell the committee what it wants to hear, but have no idea how to translate what she says into working with children in the classroom.

A trained observer understands a great deal about the teacher by just looking around the classroom. Of all possible things to emphasize what does she choose? Is everything teacher-generated with no evidence of what the students are doing? Are all the desks placed in such a way that the children cannot communicate and work with each other let alone with the teacher? Is the teacher so afraid of children and of losing control that she requires complete silence and no movement?

In watching the teacher with the class, the observer has the opportunity to note how she disciplines, how she takes into account different learning styles, how she uses cooperative learning lessons, how she presents the curriculum and in general, how she functions with the group before her. This information can only be obtained by observation, not by a verbal interview. This process results in hiring the best teachers available to teach your children and is absolutely essential.

Not all school systems give rigorous, objective teacher recruitment a high priority. In some places, it is not what you know; it is who you know that counts. Those systems often have an unspoken but understood policy of interviewing and employing only those candidates with political connections. As a result, many outstanding candidates are eliminated from consideration. The children suffer the consequences of poor teaching if less capable teachers are hired. When this happens, the recruitment process is rarely blamed, rather the children are blamed for lack of intelligence or the parents are blamed for lack of involvement.

For your children's sake it is important for you to know how teachers are chosen in your district. Since many of these decisions are made over the summer, now is the time to find out.

Teacher Tenure

Teacher tenure laws are coming under close scrutiny, usually not in a pleasant way. One headline read: "When teachers should be expelled from class." "New hope for getting rid of bad apples". The assumption seems to be that tenure permits teachers to remain in classrooms when they are "burned out" and not helpful to children.

There must be a reason why we put teachers in classrooms with a group of children and then put these classrooms together in order to make a school. The reason should be that everyone in the school is important and that all are concerned about each other. Schools are in the business of education and that should include the education of everyone involved in the enterprise. If this is not the purpose, then maybe we should consider breaking up the schools into something more efficient. If the purpose is merely to give out information so that the children can give it back correctly in tests, then maybe a more efficient operation would be to put each child in front of a computer. If this is so, then we do not need schools at all. Each child could have a computer at home.

Most people do not believe this. Schools are made up of a community of people. Every school community must decide what it is all about and what it wants to accomplish for its members. It needs to be a group decision because each member is important for the success of the others and each member has to take some responsibility for the failures.

Any group of teachers has individual strengths and weaknesses. In a safe environment, it would be okay for teachers to say what they do well and what they do not do well. In many cases, members of the school community already have this information. They know which teachers are strong in certain areas and which teachers are not.

Teachers need to be encouraged to describe their strengths and weaknesses. This information should not be used against them, but should be used to exploit their strengths and to remediate their weaknesses.

Suppose a particular school discovers that it is weak in science and math and wants to improve. The school community knows that several teachers do not like or understand these subjects. These teachers usually compensate by rigorously following the textbooks and limiting class discussions. There are options available to the school to help these teachers.

Just to mention a few: Teachers could team teach with one taking over the science and math while the other concentrates on the liberal arts. Teachers could visit classrooms where the teachers do a great job in teaching science and math. These teachers could then become mentors to those who feel insecure in these subjects. Staff development opportunities could be made available for teachers to visit other schools with outstanding programs and report back to their colleagues about what they learned. Time and money could be allocated for some teachers to take additional courses in a highly recommended science and math program. In other words, they would be helped to succeed in this educational enterprise called a school.

The may sound too "pie in the sky" to be practical but it is more practical than having a complex, expensive program of recertification which probably will not result in changing teachers or education. There has to be a more fundamental change in the system which would have a domino effect to bring about other changes.

The change necessary would have all the occupants of the school responsible for everything that happens there. This also includes the students in each individual classroom. Children are not in classrooms merely to interact individually, one-on-one with the teacher. They are part of a group brought together to help each other to learn and to grow. The same thing should be true of every adult connected with the community called school.

The Role of Administrators
in Schools

I once heard of a Symphony Orchestra whose members hired the conductor themselves and kept him as their conductor as long as he helped them to produce outstanding music. If the conductor became unable to bring out the best the orchestra had to give, they fired him. In other words, the conductor's job was to make them sound good, not the other way around. The same thing should be true of schools. The principal's job and the superintendent's job should be to make the teachers look good. Not the other way around.

The most prestigious position in education should be that of the teacher, not the principal or any other administrator. The principal ideally should be a Master Teacher chosen by the teachers he or she is to lead to better teaching. The principal should be a person of proven ability and experience who sets an example, knows how to monitor and to counsel teachers and helps them to reach the high expectations they have for themselves and their students. The principal's function should be to inspire, to motivate and to direct the staff. The ideal relationship between the principal and staff would have the principal first among peers, responsible to them and an advocate for them.

Some school systems contend that a principal does not need exposure to classroom teaching in order to function well as principal. Is the principal to be the educational leader of the school or simply a business manager whose main job is to see that supplies and services are made available within the school budget, schedules are met and forms properly filled out? A person serving in the role of principal could function adequately with only administration and management skills. However, such a person is a business manager, not a principal.

It is time we recognize that the role of principal involves two different functions: one of professional leadership, the other of administrating services. These functions might best be served by separating the one position into two. The more important and most prestigious function should be that of professional leader. It is the role that requires more training and experience and therefore higher pay. The person administrating services, however, could have many schools under his or her jurisdiction. This is a more cost efficient way to administer schools since materials bought in volume become cheaper.

Also, since most state and federal forms and requirements are the same for the district, it seems more efficient to have just one person to deal with them. This person would also oversee the buildings and grounds and in general be doing what needs to be done, within fiscal constraints, to carry out the mission defined by the educational staff. The principal and teachers should give their full attention to the main function of education: students' learning.

Making the School Building an Educational Enterprise

A twelve-month school year has the potential for bringing about many positive changes in a rigid system. One thing that would have to change is the use made of the school building. Other changes occur as teachers confer with each other and exchange ideas.

School buildings have traditionally been shut down during the summer months. This is vacation time for the staff. Normally, it is impossible to work anyhow in most of these buildings because they lack air-conditioning. During the school year, buildings are usually open from 8AM to 4PM. All of this could change if schools began to function on a twelve-month schedule. School facilities could be used to their fullest.

School buildings should be known as educational centers and be available for the educational enterprises of the whole community. The school building should be available to the community from 6AM to late in the evening, six days a week from January to December. This would require upgrading most schools not only by adding air-conditioning but also by reconfiguring space to make it more adaptable for use in different activities and by various group sizes. As things now stand, the buildings are under-utilized. The equipment, books, supplies, and material in most buildings are only used for short periods of time. Most material is discarded because it becomes obsolete rather than worn from use. Equipment is usually kept in individual classrooms and when the teachers are not there, the rooms are locked and the material sits unused.

Instead of each classroom having its own equipment, a more useful concept is a media center. The Media Center, including the Library, would house the VCR equipment, TVs, computers, books, and other materials necessary for the educational endeavor. Like the kitchen, cafeteria and gym facilities, it should be easily accessible to everyone in the building. In this way, maximum use is made of everything in the building on a year round basis.

The Educational Enterprise should be available for all ages. Pre-School children and children whose parents work should have access to it as early as 7AM and should be able to stay until 6PM. Children who require an after-school program would remain in the building under supervision of that program' staff. Senior citizens could make use of the building at times when space becomes available. When senior citizens begin coming to the Educational Building, the opportunity is available for them to see ways in which their particular skills would be helpful to the staff and the students. The offices of administrators should also be in the Educational Building. Sometimes administrators get so far away from students that they lose contact with the real world in the schools and become less effective.

Schools open all year could be reorganized for more flexibility in planning not only teachers' schedules but also students' schedules. The vacations of the students and teachers could be staggered over the year in order to make full use of the school facility.

The way is also open to reorganize the structure of classes and discard grade designations. Since the school is open twelve months, it would no longer be necessary to have the first grade, second grade and so forth. The present grade system divides time into blocks and some children fail because they cannot keep to this rigid pre-determined schedule. A better system involves individualized programs in which children advance when they have achieved mastery. Acknowledgement would, therefore, be made of differences in maturation rates, interests and learning styles.

With a twelve month school year, teachers will have time to confer with each other to consider more flexible ways to use their time and talents. Teachers, who feel comfortable with the team teaching concept, might try an arrangement where two teachers are responsible for one class. One teacher comes in the morning and the other comes in the afternoon. This type of arrangement is convenient when teachers want to have time to take courses, to observe and to train interns, and to attend professional workshops. When one teacher is out, the other teacher takes over. This and other types of arrangements guarantee continuity of instruction to the students and give the teachers the flexibility needed to accomplish their goals.

Another way to achieve flexibility is to have a group of children assigned to several teachers for a period of years or to have one teacher continue with the class. A school of 2000 children from grades five to high school in Cologne, Germany uses this system. Eighty-five to ninety students are assigned to a team of six to eight teachers. The students never experience a substitute teacher. All of the decisions are made by this teaching team: how the students will be grouped; which teachers will be assigned to which students; who will teach any subject and how many subjects will be taught each day. In addition, this team of teachers remains with the same students for six years.

When teachers are given the opportunity to communicate with each other over educational issues, they have the possibility of attempting new and potentially more successful teaching strategies. The teachers in Cologne decided to use the technique of cooperative learning in their classes. Pupils work in groups of five and six and are of mixed ability levels. There is a minimum of teacher talking and lecturing. Students are actively engaged, working on problems together, helping and learning from each other.

Another group of teachers restructured the curriculum and began the Key School. These teachers decided to tap students' multiple intelligences through the use of an interdisciplinary curriculum. The curriculum they developed is tied together by themes that span all grades and subjects which change over the course of the year. In addition the students receive instruction in the basic academic subject.

These teachers not only are using their gifts and creative talents for the good of their students, they are making teaching an exciting, vibrant and involved profession.

The introduction of the twelve-month school year has the potential for bringing changes in a rigid system that finds it difficult to change. It will cost money, of course, but so do military weapons, bail-outs of financial institutions and other changes.

Now is the time for change. Our children deserve nothing less than total commitment on our part.

Who Decided?

Who decided that the concept of middle school for children from ten to fourteen was a good idea? At the very time when children are most insecure, they are forced to leave a familiar environment where they know the teachers, their classmates, and the school to go to a new school in which they have to begin all over again.

At a time when children should be able to contribute to the school community by being leaders and top of the heap, they are made insignificant by being put at the bottom of the heap.

They are forced into a situation where they have to re-establish themselves with a group of new students, new teachers, new rules, and lots of anxiety. At this most precarious stage of their development, physically, mentally and socially, the school system gives them a double whammy by casting them adrift.

Who decided that the K-8 school was an outmoded concept and children needed to be separated from younger children when they reach preadolescence? In the K-8 school, the older children were leaders the younger ones looked up to and wanted to emulate. The K-8 school helped the older students by putting them on the student council and in general gave them opportunities to become responsible models for the younger ones. The school also crossed age lines and used older students to help younger ones to learn. Older students understood that they should not disappoint the younger ones by acting irresponsibly. It would be noticed because everyone knew them and had high expectations.

Who decided that middle school teachers could teach any subjects because they had a K-8 certification? If they are assigned to teach math, science or social studies, they do not need any extra certification in these subjects as do high school teachers. Many schools do not provide teachers with extra training when they make these assignments.

There are a lot more questions that come under the topic of "Who Decided?". Who decided that the school year should consist of 180 days out of a possible 260 days? Who decided that children should be segregated by chronological age rather than by other criteria such as: ability level, maturation level, learning style, to mention but a few? Age probably is the least valid indicator of the range of possibilities of a group.

Who decided that there is only one way to teach a subject and that administrators are the best judge of what that method should be? The whole language approach to reading as opposed to phonics is one example. Instead of teachers being expert in several approaches, they must teach one approach, and if the child cannot learn that way, he fails. No consideration is given to the fact that children have different learning styles: some are right brain learners, some are left. Some require a great deal of repetition and hands on experience, others do not. Some are auditory learners, others are visual. Some are slow to mature, others are not.

Who decided that administrators and school board members are better judges of what makes a teacher good than the teachers? Administrators and Boards give teachers life-time tenure then leave and the teachers and the school are left with the consequences of their ill-formed, often politically motivated decisions.

Who decided that teachers are qualified to practice their profession with a few months of student teaching and no internship? At least three years internship under the guidance of experienced teachers should be required before a new teacher is left on her own in the classroom.

Who decided—but I am running out of space. You can add your questions now.

Two Year Diploma

Students need to have some say in their education.

I would like to propose a use of vouchers and a two-year diploma in public education which would solve the problem of the dropout and the disruptive student.

Perhaps we are dragging the whole process out longer than is necessary or healthy. Mortimer Adler says adolescence is a pathological state, half way between being immature and being mature. Also today's children become physically mature at an age earlier than the previous generation. Suppose we shortened the whole process to two years of high school. The requirements for the diploma would change but after two years students could leave with a certificate. The next two years could be more like a junior college program.

The diploma would certify that the student can read, use correct English, knows how to verbally communicate, can write clearly, can negotiate: understands finances and basic mathematical concepts, and knows how to be a good citizen. Since he is entitled to four years of schooling, he can choose to go further, to learn a trade, be an apprentice for two more years or choose college prep courses.

When I was a counselor at a junior college in California, all students over eighteen were admitted with or without a high school diploma and it was free. There was more prestige in attending college than high school. The catch was that they had to pass tests in math and English as a prerequisite for other courses. They took remedial courses until they passed the tests. Many students never got past the remedial courses mainly because they had not used their time wisely in high school where they had been truant, unruly and often suspended. There was never a discipline problem in Junior College because they were there by choice, not by law.

Schools are places of learning for those students willing and able to learn. There is an implied contract. Teachers can teach but it is up to the student to learn. If the student, for whatever reason, is not ready to learn, then the contract is broken. Schools were not meant to be punitive institutions or holding pens to keep disruptive students off the streets.

The system could change with the use of vouchers. If a student wants to work and sees no advantage to attending school, his voucher would be returned to him to be used at a later date. If a student is disruptive and is not taking advantage of the education offered, his voucher could be returned to him to be redeemed at a later time when he is ready. The students are not labeled dropouts and they are not being punished. They are making a choice to defer their education to a time when they can profit from it.

With this system, schools get out of the business of being punitive. Students who drop out of school do not need to be labeled or punished. They are already punishing themselves by their self-destructive behavior. Instead, the students make the choice and they have a say in what happens to them. The schools merely let the consequences of the students' behavior take effect. At the same time, schools leave them with hope for the future. The opportunity is always there for them to redeem their vouchers at a later date in order to rectify a mistake they made when they were very young and very immature.

Schools may need to become more accessible in order to accommodate a different population of students under this plan. Many will be older and take longer to complete a program. Many will be working and, perhaps supporting a family. Schools would need to be open twelve months a year from morning through evening to accommodate all students.

When the student chooses to learn, at whatever age, he should find a welcome at the school and a curriculum appropriate to his needs as a learner. This use of vouchers is encouraging and positive to all students. Why not give it a try? A successful democracy requires that all its citizens have the education necessary to make informed decisions.

Uniform Approaches Nose Out Individuality

Many years ago my friend went to Hollywood to have plastic surgery done on her nose. She felt her nose was too big and she wanted movie star, Kim Novak's nose. That is what she got because, at the time, this was the ideal nose and every woman who had plastic surgery got the same nose. While my friend's new nose was smaller, it did not improve her looks which had been striking. It just made her look like every other woman who had Kim Novak's nose.

Outstanding plastic surgeons no longer do this. The object of the surgery now is to improve the unique looks of the individual person and not to make that person look like somebody else. When the surgeon is successful, people do not notice that the person's features are different; they just notice that the person looks rested and wonderful.

Plastic surgeons learned something very important. They did not have to make duplicates of some perceived ideal face, which would be boring; they could work with the face each person brought to them and improve it without changing its uniqueness. Schools could learn a lesson from this.

Each child who enters the school system is unique. Children are more unique and creative as kindergartners than they are as seniors in high school. As kindergartners, each one has a unique way of looking at problems, at solving them, at asking interesting questions, at viewing events and the world around them. They have taught themselves a great deal in five short years and arrive at school as accomplished learners, interested and curious. Most school systems, however, instead of building on this uniqueness and treating children as individuals, proceed to fit them into a uniform mold.

Schools have decided what and how a child will learn before they ever see him. Schools have a pre-determined curriculum, time-table, and evaluation schedule.

Each child gets the scholarly equivalent of Kim Novak's nose, the standard model for education. As in the case of the surgeon, who eliminated my friend's beautiful nose, the school eliminates a unique creative way of thinking in order to provide the standard model. One cannot help wonder if inept plastic surgeons, like poor school systems; give their clients Kim Novak's nose because that is the only nose they know how to make. Is it because they do not know another beautiful nose when they see it. Or could it be that they really do not want different models but clones because they are easier to handle and to categorize.

School systems, by the early introduction of workbooks, worksheets, and other fill-in-the-blanks type of learning, quickly eliminate individuality and creativity in children. Instead of rewarding imaginative questions, the school wants only the right answers. There is only one answer that goes in those blanks. Young children quickly learn the drill and stop asking questions which are not in the curriculum. One researcher noted that tests of creativity were not valid after the third grade because children no longer thought or solved problems differently. They had become clones of the standard model. Of course, this may be what schools want to produce because they and their programs are going to be evaluated by clone-type tests.

I am not sure what made the plastic surgeons realize that they should change and not give everybody the same face. Did they just become wise by themselves or did their clients become smarter and demand something different that forced them to change? Maybe we could do the same for our children. Informed parents must demand what is best for their unique children.

Schools' Programs No Excuse For Failure

I once worked with a student who I discovered had a disability in spelling. He seemed relieved when I told him this. He had felt stupid because he could not spell no matter how hard he tried to memorize the words.

Later, he showed me a composition he had written in which many words were spelled incorrectly. I asked him why he was handing in a paper with misspelled words in it. He replied that since now everyone knows he has a disability in spelling, nobody should expect him to spell words correctly anymore.

I informed him that is not how it works. Knowing he has a problem with spelling is information he must use to solve his spelling problem. He no longer has to feel dumb or defensive about his disability, but he does have to find ways to compensate for it.

He may have to look up every word in the "Bad Spellers Dictionary" when he is unsure of its spelling. He may have to use "Spell-Check" on a computer. He may need to do many things to compensate for his disability, but he may not use it as an excuse for poor spelling.

The same reasoning is true for schools. Schools now know that many of today's children are born in poverty, are abused, and or live in homes which are not intellectually stimulating. Such children come to school in poor health, with short attention spans, poor motivation, are behind their peers intellectually, and are passive learners.

Just because everyone is aware of these deficiencies, that does not mean that schools can use this information to justify their failure to educate these children. They probably cannot be taught using the same methods which work for children coming from supportive home environments. They can learn, however, with encouragement and the right programs.

Many people believe that the present educational system is adequate as long as the requisite familial and social supports are provided for the students outside of the school. They conclude that where the supports are lacking, the system does not have to change; the families do.

For complex sociological reasons, many families are unable or unmotivated to function differently. Their children, through no fault of their own, suffer the consequences of these non-existent support systems. Schools that cling to educational programs inappropriate for these children join the ranks of failed support systems.

This type of thinking allows schools to do what the boy with the learning disability did. That is to perpetuate the myth that they are not responsible for deficiencies not of their making. It is true that schools are not responsible for the deficiencies but, like the poor speller, they must use knowledge and understanding to overcome these deficiencies.

One example was a recent description of what happened to a Chicago school system in the suburbs when white students fled from the neighborhood. One social studies teacher was quoted as saying that the school declined because blacks moved into the neighborhood. He says they won't shut up in class, so now he relies on videos to do the teaching for him.

There was no indication of how he would change his style of teaching in order to reach the students in front of him. This particular teacher will not change, he will just bide his time until retirement.

If the poor speller does not develop strategies, the result will merely be misspelled words. If the school systems and teachers do not develop strategies, the result will be another generation of children condemned to poverty and ignorance.

Schools are the last hope for those children whom society and their families, for whatever reason, have failed. School systems have the potential with our encouragement and our support both financially and emotionally, to succeed where other systems have failed. We must give the children and the schools that support now.

Everything I Wasn't Ready to Learn in Kindergarten

When a child enrolls in kindergarten and becomes part of a school system with all of its rules and regulations, parents suddenly feel left out of the decision-making process. Well parents are not the only ones, it turns out. Sometimes teachers feel the same way, especially kindergarten teachers.

At one time, the teaching of reading was not permitted in kindergarten and there was a special early childhood development certificate required for kindergarten teachers. Now any teacher, many with little or no training in early childhood development, can be assigned to kindergarten. As a result, and much against the early childhood educator's advice, kindergarten programs now emphasize reading, workbooks, testing, group drill, fill-in-the blanks and color-in-the picture activities. These teacher-directed activities tend to inhibit young children's creative impulses and much of this activity is developmentally inappropriate.

The trained early childhood educator would begin her year by taking the time necessary to get to know the developmental levels of her students before introducing pre-packaged programs.

She would introduce appropriate programs only when her students had achieved a level of readiness to be successful. To achieve this level, she would spend time providing opportunities for the children to increase their socialization skills, their expressive and receptive language skills, their creative talents. She would provide access to play centers, like a store, a house or a dress-up corner, and lots of opportunities for creative art and music activities.

She would take the children on trips to the firehouse, the store, the library, the farm so that they could come back to the classroom and talk about their shared experiences. She would read and discuss stories with them. She would involve them in a great number of hands-on activities, like using different-size measuring cups to play with water. They would be able to play with sand, to sift it to feel its consistency, to make designs with it and perhaps to trace the first letter of their names with it. They would be planning and planting a garden. All activities about which they can talk, and draw something and perhaps make a class story which the teacher writes for them.

If your child seems to be upset and not enjoying kindergarten, you might talk to the teacher and explain what is happening to him. He may not be developmentally ready to be successful at the task he is asked to do. When he is ready, he will do well on the same tasks he is presently failing.

It is important to know the school's curriculum in order to supplement it or to do something different at home if you disagree with its philosophy or pace. Instead of teaching your child the alphabet or how to count to 100 at home, try to talk, to listen and to read to him. It will be time well spent since all children do better when they have a strong foundation in language.

When your child first comes home from school, do not quiz him about his academic accomplishments and go through his bag to examine his school papers. Rather, ask: Did he make a friend that day? What did he build in the play corner? What did he talk about in school? What was fun? Did he ask any questions?

Parents can best help their children by acknowledging that children mature at different rates and the rate of development is not correlated with intelligence. Parents and teachers who attempt to accelerate this rate are doing children a disservice and causing them unnecessary stress. *Remember, childhood is a journey, not a race.*

Life Long Learners

The purpose of education is not to produce students who do well on standardized tests but to produce life-long learners who enjoy learning and are successful at it. In order to accomplish this goal, children not only need to be taught the tools for learning they also need to be taught how to use these tools so that they can continue to learn with or without the supervision of adults, in or out of school. As one kindergartner put it, "I've learned how to read, now can I go home." She probably never planned on opening a book again. She had been turned off by the whole process.

Children take different roads to learning. Some go quickly, some slowly, some are right-brained thinkers some are left. No one way is better than another. They are merely different. These differences need to be recognized and accepted. Children need not be separated from each other because of these differences. If we do that, we have what Bruno Bettelheim called, "Segregation, New Style." Children need to learn how to appreciate and negotiate with all styles of learning. They need to be exposed to the experience of hearing a topic discussed and thinking, "How interesting. I never thought of it that way." At the same time, different styles and rates of learning among children should not hinder their development or their potential for creativity. We need to develop workers for the whole spectrum of jobs in our country from creative leaders to creative craftsmen. How can we do this given our diverse population? One way is to recognize that there are several types of teaching in elementary school. One type includes basic skills: reading, writing and math. Another involves the acquisition of concepts and the analysis and exchange of ideas as in the humanities, the natural and social sciences. Children can be divided into groups according to learning style and rate of learning when teaching a skill, then brought back together as a group when using the skill as a tool for learning. For example, it makes sense to break up the class into homogeneous groups according to skill level when teaching reading, but to have heterogeneous groups for cooperative learning lessons.

This philosophy holds true for gifted and talented programs. Children in the best of these programs, instead of being completely segregated, spend time with other children. However, the distribution of their time can be different. Gifted children need less time acquiring skills and learning facts and more time exchanging and analyzing ideas. They can spend some time with all of the students learning how they think and arrive at conclusions and being contributing members of this group and some time with a small group of select students like themselves. It helps also to remove the top students from the group at times because it allows the next level of students a chance to be on top.

Many children are spending most of their time at the knowledge level of learning. That is they are learning to label, to repeat, to reproduce, to list and to describe. Most students will forget this information quickly because it is not put to any practical use and is never applied or used as a tool. We want more for our students. We want them to be creative critical thinkers who use what they are learning to further their knowledge and to solve problems and answer their questions.

True Reform

Results from the New Jersey Collegiate Basic Skills Placement Test and the Scholastic Aptitude Test indicate that not only are students not improving their performance, they are regressing. Obviously educational reforms, at least in New Jersey, are not working. The reason may be that true reform does not show instant results but takes time. True reform requires a top-to-bottom overhaul not merely applying Band-Aids on failing practices already in place. Current inadequate practices have enormous inertia and are almost impossible to change.

True change gets at the root of the problem and does not merely attempt to treat the symptom. There are three places where change needs to occur to get at the root:

1. Child care programs which nurture the physical, intellectual, social and emotional development of the child from birth to age three.

2. Teacher education programs which encourage, train and nurture young people who have the desire, ability and temperament to be outstanding teachers.

3. School choice programs whereby schools give up monopoly protection which mitigates against change.

Changes in these three areas are difficult but not impossible. The good news is we do not have to start from scratch or re-invent the wheel in order to accomplish these changes. The research studies have been done and we know what works. Other countries and other states have begun to incorporate these findings into programs which are successful.

All that needs to be done is for our state to follow the leaders to help all New Jersey children as other states and countries are helping their children.

Let us start with day care. We can look to France for that program. France believes that children are a national resource and are everybody's responsibility and that the day care system is to help children to develop and thrive. There is mandated paid parental leave for childbirth and adoption. All day care providers are licensed, and receive benefits like sick leave and social security. Day care programs are visited periodically by trained pediatric nurses. Teacher turn-over is low and the providers receive good salaries and subsidized training. We have far to go to meet France's standards. Further delay can only make the task more difficult.

When children are nurtured from birth, they come to school enthusiastic, curious, creative and ready to learn the school's curriculum. They should expect to have teachers who know how to nurture these qualities. Otherwise what has been a good beginning can have a tragic end. Poor pedagogical practices produce dropouts.

Arthur Wise, President of the National Council for Accreditation of Teacher Education, gives only one example: forty percent of our math teachers did not major in math and are not certified to teach it. Most colleges require that teachers take disconnected "how to" courses, in many cases taught by professors who are not themselves master teachers. Many teacher training programs do not have a vision of the kind of teacher they want to produce and do not have a thoughtful philosophy of education based on research and sound educational practice.

Research has shown us what is needed to make our schools work for our children. It is time the citizens of New Jersey and the United States take action to demand that changes be made which get at the root of the problem. We have failed many students of this generation. Let us try to do better by the next.

Childhood

Schools and parents need to understand how children grow and develop in order to provide the best learning experiences for them. These days, most parents and schools emphasize only the cognitive development of the child. The physical, emotional and social development is not considered as important and is usually ignored even though these aspects of the child's development cannot be separated from the cognitive.

Given this trend, however, one would assume that since so much emphasis is being put on the cognitive development of children that educators and parents know what they are doing and are doing it well. This does not appear to be the case. What is actually happening is that adults are making mistakes because of this misplaced emphasis and are even forgetting some things about a child's learning that they used to know. It seems that the time is ripe to review the results of the research conducted by Dr. Jean Piaget on the cognitive development of children. He is the author of many books including "Science of Education and the Psychology of the Child."

Professor Piaget worked at the Institute Rousseau in Geneva. For much of his career, he studied one limited area of life, i.e. the spontaneous growth of the capacity for logical thinking. His concept of intelligence is biological. He believed that man, at birth, is less equipped with innate mechanisms than any other living being. This forces each person to go through a process of development which can only be done by acting on and reacting to the environment. Developing babies rapidly learn to influence their environment, to adapt it to themselves and to learn about it by exploring it. This exploratory drive, sometimes called playfulness, has a direct bearing on how the child learns.

Childhood, therefore, is not a necessary evil, but is a biologically useful phase in which the child adapts itself to a physical and social environment. Every child must experience his environment in order for learning to take place. Piaget found that children must progress through a series of stages before they attain adult intelligence. These stages are the same for everybody and a stage cannot be skipped. He believed that, if a developing person fails to complete a stage, further progress is inhibited.

Adults tend to want to get on with it and to rush children through these stages. Sometimes children are given activities which, while harmless, may be nearly useless at their stage of development. Hans Furth, a student of Piaget and author of "Piaget for Teachers", feels that the average five year old is unlikely, when forced to practice reading or writing, to engage his intellectual powers to any substantial degree. Other, less abstract activities are more appropriate to that level, and more likely to stimulate those powers. In Furth's view, the Educator's role is not to treat the child as an ignorant adult to be stuffed with facts, but to remember that the child's mind is growing and developing. The child should be provided with opportunities to form his own intellectual and moral reasoning powers by interacting physically and socially, as well as intellectually, with his environment.

In J.M. Stephens' book, "The Process of Schooling", the following proposal is made: Adopt the model of agriculture for schooling rather than that of the factory. The "factory educator" looks at schooling as an assembly line and expects that, for every innovation on the instructional assembly line, some measurable effects should appear in the product, i.e. the students coming out. In agriculture on the other hand, you do not start from scratch, and you do not direct your efforts to inert and passive materials. You start with a complex and ancient process, and you organize your efforts around what seeds, plants and insects are likely to do anyway. You do not supplant or ignore these older organic forms, you work through them. In like manner, our children embody a miraculously successful strategy of nature which we must not ignore.

What is needed is considerable sensitivity and common sense. Rousseau taught us, "Hold childhood in reverence, and do not be in any hurry to judge it for good or ill . . . Give nature time to work before you take over her task, lest you interfere with her method . . . A child ill taught is further from virtue than a child who has learned nothing."

Geniuses

Are we producing any geniuses? Geniuses are risk-takers. They put novel ideas together and see what happens. They do not seem too concerned about coming up with the "right" answer. Rather they ask the question: "What if . . ." They have not lost their child-like curiosity.

Before entering the school system, children ask lots of questions. "Why is the sky blue?" "Where do the stars come from? And why do they twinkle?" "Why does three times four equal four times three?" are just a few. Most parents can add to this list other thought-provoking questions asked by their children.

The school curricula tend to retrain children not to ask their own questions but to learn answers to the questions asked by adults. Geniuses seem to have the capacity to ignore traditional questions and to come up with new questions and their own unique answers.

There are ways for you to help your child to continue to be a questioner. Encourage but do not force your child to make the most of each impulse of curiosity. Provide a stimulating environment without the pressure to achieve. When your child expresses curiosity about something, try to gauge the depth of his interest and provide appropriate books, tools or other means for him to continue his quest to know. Then get out of his way. Do not make it your project. Curiosity should be natural, not forced. When it is forced or the child is made to feel that he is doing something unusual, the impulse may leave him.

There are children who develop specific talents early and become labeled as prodigies. These children sometimes have a difficult time as adults because their talents, while unusual in children, are not so unusual in adults. They may have become true geniuses as adults had they not been labeled exceptional at a young age.

John Stuart Mill's father brought him up to be a risk-taker and original thinker. In his autobiography, Mill says that his Father never allowed anything he learned to become an exercise in mere memory. Anything he could learn or find out by thinking he was never told. He was only told when he had exhausted all efforts to find the answer himself.

The autobiography of the physicist, Richard Feynman, talks about how his father educated him. When they went for walks, his father never had him memorize the names of all of the trees and plants, rather he asked him to describe what he saw with his eyes and what he felt with his own senses.

A study of children who were exceptional in math found the following characteristics: they were quick to generalize; they were flexible in their thinking and could change easily from one process to another; they were not bound by techniques that had been successful in the past and so could change to other techniques when these failed; they looked for simple, direct, elegant solutions; they could easily reverse their train of thought.

Think of your child's school program. Is it helping him to become this kind of creative thinker? If it is not, you might want to provide the appropriate atmosphere in your home. Such an atmosphere should help him to develop those characteristics which are useful not only for traditional academic skills but for handicrafts, the arts, the trades and daily life.

A child is never helped by being pushed to do things before he is developmentally ready to do them. Rather, he is helped by being encouraged to ask questions both at home and at school and to have his questions acknowledged. He is helped by being encouraged to be curious about the world about him. He is mostly helped by being encouraged to be an active learner and not just a passive observer.

If you have nurtured your child to become this kind of learner and thinker, you should monitor his school program to ensure that what you have begun continues.

Finally, good teachers require school systems which encourage and nurture their talents.

Special Education

The law states that in order to serve the needs of special education children there must be a Child Study Team available to every school. The core team members include a school psychologist, a learning consultant and a social worker. Three highly trained people in complementary disciplines.

The school psychologist has the expertise to develop programs both for staff and students that would deal with situations before they became problems. The learning consultant has the expertise to work with students and staff to enhance the learning process. The social worker has the expertise to work with students and staff to promote social awareness among and between groups. All of this training and talent is going to waste because special education is overwhelmed with rules and regulations.

There are only two things most child study team members have time to do under the law: test and fill out forms according to a rigid schedule. These required tasks take up so much time that there is none left to make even these activities meaningful.

Bureaucracies only believe in numbers. They really do not care what the numbers mean or what use is made of them. They want everything documented and reported. The resulting reports go in a file and stay there because there is no time for anybody to look at them and really understand them.

Bureaucracies trust nobody to act competently. Members of child study teams know what programs are good for children. They do not need to do exhaustive mandated testing or to assign labels to know this. They need only to work out appropriate programs with competent teachers. The most thorough testing, the most beautiful reports, the most wonderful recommendations are pointless without competent teachers.

It is not necessary to second guess the capable teacher by constant evaluations of the child. After the child has been in the class over a period of time, the teacher knows him better than anybody else in the school. She can make the best recommendations for on-going programs. Test results are not as reliable as the opinion of a good teacher.

Mandated special education requirements have grown by leaps and bounds. These proliferating rules are a burden to the child study team because they make demands on its limited time. They are a burden to the school system because they make demands on its limited funds. If the state does not take action soon, special education is going to, as the expression goes, "kill the goose that laid the golden egg". Schools are going to balk at funding it.

Child study team members know that they have more to offer children than they are able to under the present mandates. It is time for the state department of education to consult them before more rules and regulations are added to an already overwhelmed child study team and all special education programs suffer.

Moral and Intellectual Autonomony

Once, at a school conference, I asked his teacher if my son was empathetic. "If he sees a classmate in difficulty, does he try to help?" "Does he express concern if a classmate is hurt?" "If another child needs help with his classwork, does he offer assistance?" She said she did not know because the children in her class were required to stay in their seats and were not permitted to talk. She emphasized the words "her class" and never referred to it as "our class".

Why do we continue to put children in a classroom together? The reason should be that children learn as much from each other as they do from the teacher—maybe more. They are intellectually stimulated by each other. They learn from the different ways of thinking of their classmates. They recognize and accept different learning styles.

Often, when a child makes a mistake, the teacher says "That's wrong." and asks another child for the "correct" answer. She can be much more helpful to the whole group if she says, "That's interesting. How did you arrive at that answer?"

The child's explanation usually will reveal some correctable misconception, but sometimes it may indicate that he is a divergent, creative thinker who sees things differently from the rest of the group. Understanding how such a student thinks would be interesting and helpful to everyone in the class. It also helps students to understand that there is more than one way to solve a problem.

Teachers, who insist that their students remain silent and immobile, tend to teach mainly by the lecture method. They stand in front of the class and do most of the talking. Usually, when they do interact, it is with one child at a time. Social Interaction and cooperative learning are discouraged. In classes run like this, little would be lost if the school system broke up the class and isolated each student in front of a TV monitor.

In such a system, the teacher gives lectures from a TV studio. The children interact with her, one at a time by pushing buttons and turning on query lights. The teacher then selects one of the lights and opens a channel for the question. The students do not interact with each other. This eliminates students talking and moving around which some teachers find threatening to their authority. This is not as far-fetched as it sounds; it is already being done where necessary to serve widely separated rural communities which have few children.

Teachers who keep tight control of their class and who do not permit, encourage and plan for interactions among the students not only waste valuable learning experiences, they retard the children's progress toward their full intellectual potential. It reminds me of a cartoon where the teacher says to the class: "This class will stimulate your ideas and thoughts . . . and remember, no talking." We all perceive how ridiculous this sounds and know instinctively that there will be little learning or creative thinking in that class.

A class is comprised of a group of people who work together for a common goal and are concerned about each other. The whole class, which includes the teacher, is involved and responsible not only for the successes of the group but for its failures. They all succeed and fail together. The students not only develop intellectually by learning together, they also grow morally by developing a concern for their peers. Children learn concern for others by observing and modeling adult behavior and by helping and working with each other.

Jean Piaget, the noted Swiss psychologist, stated that the aim of education is moral and intellectual autonomy. They go together. Everything we do in the name of education should have the potential for developing these two attributes in our children. Anything we do in the name of education which thwarts the development of these attributes should be re-evaluated and changed.

The Joy of Learning

There once was a great deal of press given to a comparison of the educational systems of our country and Japan. The results of a study entitled, "Japanese Education Today" praised the high level of overall academic achievement of the typical Japanese student. This level was achieved through a combination of high expectations, hard work, well-rewarded teachers and the heavy involvement of Japanese mothers in the education of their children.

The Japanese and perhaps the Chinese seemed to have no question about the purpose of education: it is to do well on standardized tests. In order to do well, knowledge needs to be conveyed by the teacher to the student. It is up to the student to remember what he has been taught so that he can answer the questions on the test. The ultimate goal is to be admitted to the most prestigious university. Once admitted, the students tend to relax and do not need to excel because they have already achieved their goal. The Japanese also admit that an emphasis on knowing the one right answer on the test, leads to conformity and lack of creativity.

The Japanese students are being taught that the purpose of education is to pass tests. The purpose of education in America ideally has been to make life-long learners of the students.

Hopefully, we would like to produce students who learn because there is an intrinsic value in simply finding an answer to a question. There should be some joy in the activity. In Japan, the joy seems to be in pleasing adults or in knowing you are the best test taker, or in knowing you can relax and enjoy yourself

Children will only become life-long learners if they take pleasure in the activity and they feel there is some useful purpose to it. Otherwise, they will stop as soon as they are left unsupervised. This is happening more and more. When children have a choice, they do not read a book, they watch television. We seem to forget that what we learn should be put to some use. We never seem to use our learning as a tool in order to take the next step or in order to find an answer. The child who does is our creative child. He learns because he wants to know and not because it is required. This attitude should be what we foster in all children.

A parent once came to me because she was anxious to know her son's reading level. I suggested she give him a book and listen to him read. She said he never opens a book. My comment was that showed her that he was a non-reader no matter what the test score indicates. Another parent complained that her child never reads at home and she felt it was the teacher's responsibility to make him read. I asked her if her son ever saw her husband or her reading. She said no because they did not have time and besides she did not enjoy reading.

While learning is hard work, children need to take some pleasure and joy in learning in order for it to have meaning and in order for what they learn to be put to use. Adults can be most helpful to children by modeling behavior which indicates that they learn because of the pleasure they get from learning and not because of the prestige involved or because someone else will notice and give them praise.

Science Literacy

A teacher informed a parent that her young son would be taken out of the regular class for short periods in order to receive extra help in reading. The parent expressed concern that her son would be missing something in the regular class. The school informed the parent that he would not miss things like recess, art or music. He would only miss science. Everybody, that includes parent, teacher, and child was satisfied with this arrangement. All agreed that the student, by missing the science program, would not miss anything important to his education.

Albert Shanker lamented the fact that our students, and that includes all of our outstanding students, perform less well on standardized tests as their counterparts in other countries. The students' scores were compared in math and science since they are the only ones that lend themselves to comparison among cultures. The conclusion seems to be that either our students, or our educational system or both are inferior to those in other countries.

Another and perhaps more reasonable explanation may be that many of our students receive no education in math and science at all. Other countries, in addition to having a longer school year, begin implementing an earnest science and math curriculum in the first grade. Math is taught together with science since math is the tool of science. We tend to teach subjects in isolation with no connection to the real, technological world the children are living in.

Nancy Devlin, PhD

We are missing a golden opportunity by not learning from the success of other countries. Children are born scientists. They are naturally curious about every new thing they observe. Most are quickly discouraged from this curiosity and creativeness because nobody seems interested in their questions. By third grade, they do not ask: "Why is the sky blue?" "What makes grass green?" "Why does the light stop when I turn off the switch?" They just fill in the blanks in answer to adult's questions. Only a few cling to that precious inquisitiveness.

Nobel Prize winner, Leon Lederman, says: "Scientists are children who never grew up." Like Peter Pan they see magic in the way the natural world is put together. They delight in exploring. We may be denying our children this experience by the way we teach science or by not teaching math and science at all.

The problem may stem from the fact that many of our teachers are themselves victims of a poor science and math curriculum and feel uncomfortable teaching these subjects. That could be remedied by staff development programs for all elementary school teachers. Every teacher should know enough science so that she or he is equipped to answer children's questions or at least to be able to say, "Let's find out" and know how to do that.

The American Association for the Advancement of Science released the results of a four year study of science education in the public schools. In their study, "Benchmarks for Science Literacy" they recommend that children as young as five be given regular science lessons—not just scattered experiments like collecting snowflakes and learning that each snowflake has six points—but lessons given as often as reading. The study found that typical prevailing techniques require memorization, for example memorizing the 109 elements on the periodic table, rather than devising and testing theories or drawing conclusions from experimental data. The study makes no recommendations on national testing for fear that schools and teachers would take the recommended benchmarks for each grade and use them as test questions. Children should be learning science not just to pass tests, but to develop curiosity and understanding of the world around them.

The parent who did not object to having her son taken out of the science lesson in order to receive more help in reading probably was making the correct choice given the state of the present science curriculum in our schools. There will be no more American Nobel prize winners in science and perhaps no more American scientists unless we change our attitude towards science and math education.

Auditory Processing

If your child is failing in school and had ear problems as a baby, the difficulty may be due to poor auditory processing. This impairment seems to affect boys more than girls.

Some children cannot screen out conflicting noises and miss much of what is said. This problem often goes undetected because they can hear in a one-on-one situation when the adult looks right at them, but fail to get the message when competing sounds interfere. They cannot seem to ignore distractions.

A Central Auditory battery of standardized tests may be in order especially if you constantly describe your son as a child who never listens to anybody. Even without testing, however, you can begin to help your son if you suspect there is a problem.

Get his full attention before speaking to him. Stoop down to his level and make eye contact. When you are sure you have his full attention; make your sentences and requests short and concise. Then ask him to repeat back to you what you have just said to him. Do not talk to him when he has his back to you. He will not understand what you have said and you will both end up angry and frustrated.

You can help him to increase his ability to attend and to disregard distractions by means of games. One game might be to ask him to carry out a series of verbal commands in sequence. If he follows the sequence correctly, he wins the game and the prize. For example:" John there is something hidden in the third drawer of the bureau on the right side." "Find it and bring it to me." For other ideas for listening games, ask your librarian. Also, look for games for Christmas presents which involve listening and following directions.

Many elementary teachers make adjustments to their teaching style almost automatically when the child has difficulty processing information. They get the child's attention first and have him repeat the direction given. Middle school teachers, however, tend not to do this. In middle school, there are more teachers with more classes and more children to get to know.

These teachers tend to lecture while walking up and down the aisle. Children with processing problems miss most, if not all, of what is said. That is why this problem may not manifest itself until middle school.

Auditory processing problems do not necessarily mean a child has ear problems. The difficulty has to do with the brain not the ear. Any ear problems, once discovered, were probably corrected as a baby. In the meantime, however, the baby did not hear well when the "window of opportunity" for learning expressive and receptive language was open.

There are other children, however, who do have undiagnosed ear defects. Be concerned if your child is not disturbed by loud noises; does not respond when spoken to; uses gestures almost exclusively to establish needs rather than verbalizing; watches adults' faces intently; his attention wanders while someone is reading to him; often says "huh" or "what" indicating he does not understand; he breathes with his mouth open.

When hearing problems go undetected, children have problems in school which are usually attributed to other reasons. These children are restless, have short attention spans, are distracted in groups, and are seldom first to do what the teacher asks. In addition, they are unaware of social conventions like automatically saying, "thank you.", "I'm sorry". They grab another child to get his attention rather than saying his name and, in general, is unaware of disturbing others with noises.

Children with hearing problems may not be able to communicate or to use words as effectively as their peers. As a result they may appear to be less intelligent than they really are. When tested, they may do poorly because they do not understand the questions and may guess or say "I don't know." This appears to confirm the hypothesis of limited intelligence.

These children often have behavior problems because they are not sure what is expected of them.

Since most hearing problems are correctable, either through operations or hearing aids or education, it is important that parents be vigilant to catch them early.

Bullying

Most adults become incensed when they discover that there is bullying in their child's school. Immediately they advocate severe punishment of the bully. Now, who is the bully? As Pogo said, "We have met the enemy and he is us."

Severe punishments, policing and strict rules restricting their behavior will not cause bullies to relinquish their roles.

Such actions confirm them. These techniques merely put adults in the role of bullies. A much better approach, which also has the added advantage of modeling problem solving techniques, is for the adults to acknowledge that there is a problem and to work to develop programs aimed at solutions and prevention.

Schools are in the business of education. That means the education of all students including the bullies. One solution is to provide activities where students are given the opportunity to get to know each other and to learn how to interact in constructive ways.

One of the best ways to do this is through cooperative learning lessons. In the school setting, to complete assignments cooperatively, students must function as a "cooperative group". They must interact with each other, share ideas and materials, help each other learn, pool their information and resources, use division of labor when appropriate, integrate each member's contribution into a group product and facilitate each other's learning. As a result, communication, conflict management, and leadership skills are developed and in the process the students are given the opportunity to appreciate and to understand each other better.

Margaret Mead made the point that the future quality of human life, as well as the survival of the human species, will be dependent upon cooperative behavior along with a concern and respect for the rights of others. This behavior can be modeled, taught and nourished in the classroom.

Another solution involves providing opportunities for children to learn to empathize with each other. Bullies will only relinquish their dominance gained at the expense of others by the development of higher values such as empathy and consideration.

One way to do this is to help bullies feel what their victim feels. This can be done by the teacher listening to the victim in private and then conveying to a small group of his peers, which includes the bully, the distress of the victim. The teacher conveys to the group that they are not there to be blamed but for each member to offer to do something to help the victim feel better. This enables bullies to understand the extent of someone else's pain, which in severe cases, can lead to suicide. Some bullies are in so much pain themselves that they do not comprehend the pain they cause in others.

There are many other activities the school can institute to develop empathy in children. Students could be given the opportunity to help younger ones by reading to them. Older students could help others through leadership positions like being on a school council or being on the school patrol. Students could learn about those less fortunate than themselves through clothing drives, visits to nursing homes, or donating food to help the homeless. Teachers could stress empathy by such questions during the reading lesson as: "How do you think the person in the story feels?" "How would you feel if the same thing happened to you?" "What would you do to help that person?"

If there is bullying in your child's school, do not accept the school's position that it is normal and the school cannot do anything about it anyway. Something can and should be done not only for the victim's sake but for the bully's sake. Successful young bullies tend to grow up to become the hardened criminals who keep our jails full.

Encouragement

The most important thing you can do for children is to encourage them. Parents, teachers, and other adults who have children in their care need to understand an important principle of human behavior, i.e. children function best when they believe in themselves and know that other people believe in them also.

We need to believe in children and accept them as they are. The first step is to stop discouraging them by eliminating negative comments about them. We do not have to accept children's misbehavior but we should never say anything negative about them as people. We must learn to separate the deed from the doer.

Children should be helped to feel good about themselves. We do this by focusing on their strengths. This is never accomplished by telling them they can do better since that is a negative statement on what they have already done.

Some adults even manage to turn encouraging statements into discouraging ones: "It looks like you really worked hard on that . . . so why not do that all of the time?" Or "See what you can do when you really try?"

Encouragement is the prime motivator. Dr. Don Dinkmeyer, who has developed three programs based on Alfred Adler's philosophy, makes a useful distinction between praise and encouragement.

The basic difference between praise and encouragement is that praise is based on competition and is a value judgment while encouragement focuses on the effort and accepts children as they are.

Praise is for things well done. It is a reward and the child is valued by the adult. "You're a good boy." "You came in first. That's great." "I'm so proud of you."

Some children begin to rely on praise and only perform if they receive it. They may also begin to feel worthwhile only if they are on top which usually means at the expense of others. These children eventually may set unrealistic standards for themselves and learn to fear failure and refuse to take risks.

Words of encouragement, on the other hand, allow you to respond to a wide range of behavior. You focus on their strengths and assets. The words of encouragement are: "I have confidence in your judgment." "It looks as if you worked very hard on that." "I like the way you handled that." "How do you feel about that?"

Sometimes, when a child expresses discouragement, you might respond with: "Since you are not satisfied, what do you think you can do so that you will be pleased with it?" "You are making progress." "Looks like you are moving along." "You may not feel you have reached your goal, but look how far you have come."

Do not dwell on children's shortcomings, rather point out what they do right. Give help in the form of suggestions and be specific when possible. Encouragement does not compare one child with another and can be given when children feel bad about themselves and are down on themselves. We can focus on children's contributions and show we appreciate what they do for us.

Many of our children are discouraged, and discouraged children have difficulty learning. Adults who work with children need to have it within their power to counteract this. Children need and respond to encouragement. It takes practice to learn to be encouraging mainly because we have high standards for ourselves and the children in our

Nancy Devlin, PhD

care but, once learned it becomes automatic. I encourage you to try it, and I promise you will be astounded with the results.

I suggest you begin practicing by encouraging yourself, then you family. The next group that needs encouragement is teachers. Parents tend to communicate with the superintendent and School Board when they are dissatisfied, not when they are satisfied. This can be very discouraging to teachers. The next time you plan on giving a gift to a teacher or in some other way want to show your appreciation, write a letter to the teacher and send copies to the superintendent and the School Board. This is very is appropriate, very encouraging, and rarely done.

Does Your Child Really
Have ADHD?

I just returned from John's graduation from high school. Not only did he graduate in 4 years, he received two blue ribbons for his sculptures, first honors as a senior and acceptance in to college to study graphic design. Pretty good for a kid who in first grade was diagnosed by the school system as having Attention Deficit Hyperactive Disorder (ADHD).

This is a cautionary tale for all parents who have a child so designated by the school system.

It is easier for the school system to put a label on a child and make it the child's problem, rather than the school examining its philosophy and possibly discovering that it is the school system's problem. By calling it the child's problem the system does not have to change to fit the child's educational needs. Instead the child must change to fit the system's needs.

You may say that the system does not know what the children's needs are. With all of the testing and evaluations done on children, the system does have the necessary data. The problem is nobody is in charge of interpreting them and making the necessary adjustments. It is somewhat like the dilemma facing the CIA and FBI. They had all the information and data needed to predict and to thwart terrorist strikes but nobody knew how or was assigned to correlate and to interpret the information.

This is also true of special education programs. The law requires reams of testing but few people are trained and given the responsibility to correlate, to understand and to make practical use of all the data.

John's history, to which the school had access, indicated that he had frequent ear infections as a baby and subsequently had tubes in his ears. He still was not talking at age three. When he did begin speaking, he mispronounced words and nobody understood him.

In first grade, John was placed in a small class of sixteen children because they all had communication problems. These children were taught using the reading program mandated for use by the whole school. It required that every student be taught by learning the sounds of the letters and then sounding out the words. This was something, since birth, John could not do. Consequently, although bright, he was not learning to read and he knew it.

The sixteen children in his class were not permitted to move from or in their seats. They were not permitted to talk. They were not even permitted to sound out the words while working in their workbooks because that too was regarded as talking.

The teacher taught the reading lesson to the whole class as a group strictly following the teacher's manual. She worked from the chalk board at the front of the room, away from the students. John was in a seat which not only made it difficult to hear the teacher but to see the chalkboard. He had to move in his seat in order to see the board.

Because John was not learning to read, the teacher referred him to the child study team. Before he was evaluated, the school counselor called his mother and told her that John was a DSM III-R attention-deficit, hyperactive-disorder (ADHD) child. She recommended to his mother that she take him to a neurologist because there could be a question of medication. Again, something was wrong with the child, not the program the child was in.

Testing indicated that John had high average intelligence, but had a problem with language. Since the system would not change its school-wide mandated reading program, John would have to change. The only other option the school could offer was for him to receive his reading instruction in the more flexible program in the learning disability class. Since this was not acceptable under the rules and regulations for the handicapped, the school was forced to create a Resource Room Program for students like John who required reading programs appropriate for their individual learning styles. John learned to read. Thus, his story had a happy ending.

You can have a happy ending for your child if you to learn to ask questions of the school system. Here is a partial list:

If the school system labels your child, ask for a description of the behavior that results in that label. One person's definition may not be another's. This is particularly true of the ADHD label which is often based on rating scales and checklists supplied by the teacher. Observation, not checklists, is the essential procedure necessary to describe this behavior.

Ask the question, "Why". Why does the child behave that way? For some children like John, he knows he's not doing well, but he does not know why or what to do about it. He might even begin to doubt his ability to do anything right. Or he might feel that he is not a good person because he is unable to do the school work, and he is letting his parents down. He might even be afraid of losing their love.

Remember these are children. They think and interpret their world and their place in it like children, not adults. They are concrete thinkers, not abstract. They need all the encouragement and support and understanding you can give them. Your role is to be their advocates and best friends.

There are a few children for whom medication might be indicated. Before you reach that conclusion, however, be sure you understand your child's role as a member of a very complex school system.

Finally, good teachers require school systems which encourage and nurture their talents.

About The Author

Dr. Nancy Devlin graduated from Hunter College with a degree in English and a Masters degree in Guidance and School Counseling. She taught elementary school in New York City, and in military-dependent schools in Germany, Denmark and Japan. She earned her Ph.D. in Educational Psychology at the University of California at Berkeley. She was a psychologist for twenty-two years in the Princeton Schools. She is a licensed psychologist, a family therapist and a nationally-certified school psychologist. She is married to a Physicist and they have three sons. She has published hundreds of newspaper articles on issues of education and childrearing. At present, she has a website and blog, www.Cassandrasclassroom.com providing information on education, parenting and related topics.